THE STRAY CAT I FEED

我喂养的野猫

🐾 Mandy Oren 🐾

美國紐約龍出版社
Long Publishing Corp.

ISBN: 978-1-953903-10-5
First Published in New York by Long Publishing Corp.
First Paperback Edition: April 2024
The stray cat I feed of Poetry with Mandy Oren

《我喂养的野猫》 Mandy Oren　著

編輯策劃：胡桃
裝幀設計：吳言

美國龍出版社出版發行
出　版　人：Sonia Hu
版　　　次：2024 年 4 月紐約第一版，第一次印刷
國際書號：978-1-953903-10-5

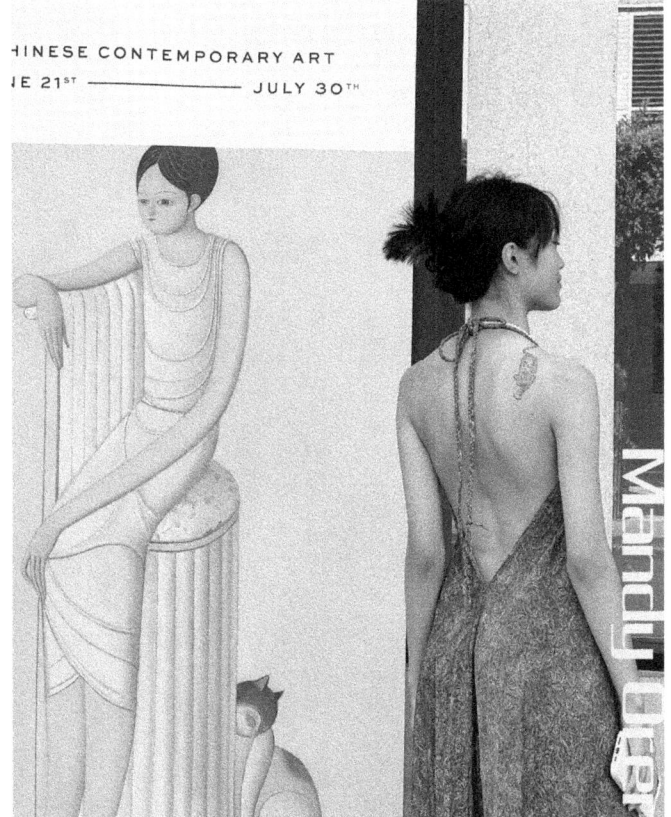

目录 / CONTENTS

我喂养的野猫　/ 08

母亲　/ 12

春天　/ 16

小时候　/ 20

我的名字　/ 24

小老虎　/ 28

青莲寺　/ 32

一尘不染　/ 36

古巴　/ 38

幸福　/ 40

与水有关

　1. 杭州之初　/ 48

　2. 曼哈顿的湖　/ 52

　3. 特拉维夫的海　/ 56

今天会下雨　/ 60

在沙漠　/ 64

酒吧　/ 66

宠物的命运　/ 70

我怕认错你　/ 74

西瓜　/ 78

明月　/ 80

我也会老去　/ 82

三天　/ 86

所有人，都曾经如此　/ 90

The stray cat I feed / 10

Mom / 14

Spring / 18

When I was young / 22

My Name / 26

Little Tiger / 30

Temple / 34

Spotless Mind / 37

Cuba / 39

Happiness / 44

With Water

1. Hangzhou / 50

2. Manhattan / 54

3. Tel Aviv / 58

Will it rain today / 62

In the desert / 65

BAR / 68

Life of Pets / 72

I'm afraid of mistaking you / 76

Watermelon / 79

Bright Moon / 81

I will also grow older / 84

3 days / 88

Everyone was like this once / 94

我喂养的野猫

我叫你，kk
半夜
起风了　我想你
你睡在哪里
风声很响
落叶哗哗

我醒着
竖起耳朵
顺着风声
去寻你的声音

后院
有条小巷
风在小巷里奔跑
你躲在哪里? kk

风里似乎有你的声音
在某个角落里

很遥远
很自由
你习惯了风
你习惯黑暗

我醒着
想象你在黑暗中的眼睛

黑漆漆的一片
你在夜风里
眼睛里闪着光
闪着
自由

因此
我爱你

The stray cat I feed

I call you，kk.
It's midnight,
It's windy,
I miss you.
Where are you sleeping?
The wind is loud.
Leaves rustling.

I'm awake,
Ears pricked.
Listening to the wind,
Looking for your sound.

In the backyard,
There is an alley.
The wind is running in the alley.
Where are you hiding? kk

The wind seems to carry your voice.

Resting in some corner,
Far away,
Carefree.

Used to the wind,
Used to the shadows.

I'm awake,
Thinking about your eyes in the night.

A pitch-black night,
Winds blow against your coat,
Glistening eyes,
Glowing,
Freedom

Therefore,
I love you.

母亲

放学
走一段路
然后再坐地铁
再走一段路
回家，敲门

母亲的
拖鞋声，
吧哒吧哒
从书房到客厅

门开了
我和母亲
在打开的门前
相遇

她问：你在学校
会想家么
我回：不想
只有放学时
才知道我要去坐地铁
回家

母亲将一颗金黄色的

橘子
放在我的手心
她说
我想你
母亲！

我走向我的房间
她走向厨房

母亲打开冰箱
"晚上想吃什么"
母亲问
"我不知道"
我回

我关上房门
戴着耳机
我在
我的世界
母亲——
仍站在厨房里
为我精心准备
一道
"我不知道"的
菜肴

Mom

After school,
On the subway,
Off the subway,
Back home.

Knock-knock.
Mom's slippers,
Pit pat pit pat
From the bedroom,
Across the hallway,
to the living room.

The door opened,
Mother and I,
At the open door,
encountered.

She asked: Did you miss me at school?
I replied：
I only realize,
I need to go home,
After stepping foot on the subway.

Mom placed an orange,

14

In my palm.
  "I miss you,"
She said.

Mom!

I walk to my bedroom.
She walks to the kitchen.

Opening the fridge,
  "What do you want for dinner?"
Mom asked.
  "I don't know,"
I replied.
I close the bedroom door,
Putting on my headphones.
Traveling to
A world of my own.

Mother——
Still in the kitchen,
Preparing
The dinner "I don't know".

春天

四月，
我们去了老集市
买了面包
以及鲜花

还有
白叶咸味(white leaved savory)
salvias(鼠尾草)
mint (薄荷)
Aloysiatriphylla (柠檬马鞭草)
Oregano(牛至草)
……

我们将它们
种在院子里

妈妈说
它们都是草药

每天上学前
我给它们浇水

就像给野猫喂食一样

失眠的母亲
睡觉前
喜欢吃
院子里长出来的
草药

她说：
这是
春天的礼物

Spring

March,
We went to the fair,
Bought bread,
And flowers.

and
white leaved savory
salvias,
mint,
Aloysiatriphylla (Lemon verbena),
And oregano (Oregano grass),
...

We welcomed them home,
and planted them in the yard

Mother said,
  "They are all herbs."

Every day before school,
I water them.

It's like feeding a wild cat.

Before sleeping,
Before bed,
Mother likes to take herbal medicine,
That sprouts in the backyard.

She said:
This
Is the gift of spring

小时候

小时候
我在太阳底下，奔跑
在雨中玩耍
在黄昏里
迷路

我赤着脚
走在院子里
看到
熟透的苹果，
光在树叶上
风在耳边

小时候
世界是
妈妈嘴里的故事
生活是
外婆的菜
外公的麻将

后来，有了

幼儿园
老师
同学
有了App
有了游戏

再后来，有了
自己的日记
秘密
梦想
追求

小时候
便成了回忆

When I was young

In my childhood,
I was
Hopping, charging, flying,
wherever the sunlight shines.
Playing, dancing, messing around,
wherever the rain drops and roads align.

I was getting lost,
Inside the twilight sky.
Getting lost,
In the twinkles of the stars that soared above,
Like an amalgam of bright fishes in a deep sea.
Getting lost,
In the sky's revelations.

tiptoeing,
Around the garden.
Seeing, observing,
The ripened apples.

Watching the sunlight bouncing off the fruit tree leaves,
Leaving behind a flush of soft golden glow.
Feeling the wind that blows against my perked ears,
Whispering to me the wondrous secrets of the earth.

When I was young,
The world was just
stories from mother.
Life was just
grandma's cooking,
And Grandpa's mahjong.

Then,
There was
kindergarten,
Teachers,
Classmates,
games.

Later,
There was
My own diary,
Secrets,
Dreams,
Passions.

  "Childhood"
became
just a memory.

我的名字

同学叫我
Mandy
身份证是
Zhiman
妈妈叫我
宝贝

我的名字
被不同的人说起
有着完全不同的含义

如果让我选择
我希望

Zhiman
是可以持续而缓慢的生长的
名字
像一本厚厚的书

Mandy
是友善平和正直的

名字

宝贝
是一个值得被爱
也懂得去爱的
名字

My Name

My friends call me
Mandy.
My passport says
Zhiman
My mom calls me
baby

My name,
When called by different people,
Has different meanings.

If I could choose,
Then I hope

Zhiman
Is a name
That is able to grow and flourish,
Like a thick book

Mandy
Is a name

That is kind and righteous.

Baby
Is a name
That deserves to be loved,
And understands how to love.

小老虎

我织过
一只粉色的
小老虎
偷偷地
是母亲节的
惊喜

我画过
许多颜色的
小老虎
它们快乐地
生活在纸上
是记忆

我养过
一只黄色的小猫
在以色列Jaffa老城的
后院
我每天蹲下身去喂它
叫它
小老虎

我想
纹一只小老虎

在后脖子
或者
在手腕
也可以在
有心脏的左胸

她很爱
小兔子
她的电脑上贴着
一只小兔子和一根小红萝卜
因为她的妈妈
属兔
而她
属虎

以前
我抬头望她
她是一只
又高又勇敢的大老虎
现在
我低头看她
她变成一只
又矮又孩子气的小老虎

Little Tiger

I' ve secretly crocheted
A pink,
Little tiger.
As a surprise
For Mother' s Day.

I' ve drawn
Little tigers,
Of all colors of the rainbow.
Living on,
Happily,
On the paper,
As memories.

I' ve taken care of
A little orange cat,
In a garden,
in Yafo.
Everyday,
I feed it,
Pet it,
And call it,
Little tiger.

I think,

I should crochet a little tiger
To wear as a scarf,
On my neck.
Or,
As a bracelet,
On my wrist.
Also, A pin,
To wear on my heart.

She really loves bunnies.
On her laptop,
Sticks a little rabbit holding a carrot.
Because her mom
Is a rabbit.
But mine
Is a tiger.

Before,
When I had to raise my head to look at her,
She was a tiger.
Tall and brave and a big tiger.
Now,
I lower my head,
And she turns into a
Cute, short, and still brave little tiger.

青莲寺

赤脚踩在木板上
咯吱咯吱
母亲说
就像回到童年时
外婆家
一样安心

跪下来
很低
眼睛可以看到
树根
以及佛像

席地而坐
听雨
听风

看庭前
树枝上挂着的
雨珠

满庭子的青苔
绿成
一座山
一条河
一片海

Temple

Barefoot stepping on the wooden planks
creaking
 creaking
Mother says
It's like returning to childhood
Grandma's house
A place of solace
Kneeling down
Very low
Eyes catching sight of
Tree roots
And the Buddha statue

Sitting on the ground
Listening to the rain
Listening to the wind
Observing the courtyard

Raindrops hanging from
Branches

The moss—filled courtyard
Greening into
A mountain
A river
A sea.

一尘不染

高楼
樱花

蜘蛛网状的地铁
世界最繁忙的
十字路口

精致的庭院
幽静的寺院

茶道
花道
哲学小道

无处
不
一尘不染

Spotless Mind

Tall buildings,
Cherry blossoms.

A spiderweb−like
Subway,
The world's busiest
Intersection.

Exquisite courtyards,
Serene temples.

Tea ceremonies,
Flower arrangements,
Philosophical pathways.

Nowhere
that's not
Spotless.

古巴

哈瓦那很繁华很
破旧

公园里面坐满了刮卡的人
从邮局里买来的限量版 Wi-Fi卡

老旧公寓旁边的店铺前
排了长长的队伍
拿票 兑换食物的人
只有土豆和面粉
满街都是漂亮的
老汽车
50年代的就像一首道华丽的
老歌

到处都有浓郁的
雪茄冒着气泡的 啤酒
每个角落里都充溢着
野猫的
呼唤

Cuba

Havana,
Very
Prosperous,
Yet
Dilapidated.

In the park,
Seats occupied
By people scratching Wi-Fi cards
Purchased from the post office.

In front of the shops beside the old apartments,
Long queues form,
Ticket holders exchange for food,
Only potatoes and flour available.

Beautiful
Old cars
From the 50s,
Resemble a magnificent
Old song.

Everywhere,
Rich Cigars,
Bubbling Beer,

Every corner,
Overflowing with
The calls of
Stray cats.

幸福

母亲说
去跑步
去冲浪
去博物馆
这样
你会幸福

我说
你别烦我
我只想
睡觉

我躲在浴缸里
上网
母亲敲门
我大喊
别烦我

母亲站在浴室门外：
你在我的肚子里

住了九个月
那个时候
我很幸福

我回：
你很幸福
而那个时候
我什么都不知道

我用猫粮
喂熟一只猫
我幸福
猫不一定
幸福

我用礼物
与顺从
成了某人的朋友
我幸福
某人说

我不知道

我在海边奔跑
海水打湿了我的裤子
下雨了
雨水
打湿了
我的眼睛

我全身湿透
推开家门
听到
母亲打破了
手里的碗
铛的声音
吓人一跳

母亲说
打破
是好事

桌子上
有准备好的晚餐
我吃了很多
母亲说，
看你吃我做的饭
我觉得幸福

我终于
回道：
我也幸福

Happiness

Mother says,
Go for a run,
Go surfing,
Visit a museum,
That way,
You'll be happy.
I say,
Don't bother me,
I just want
to sleep.

I hide in the bathtub,
Online,
Mother knocks on the door,
I shout,
Don't bother me.

Mother stands outside the bathroom:
You lived in my belly
for nine months,
Back then,

I was happy.

I reply:
You were happy,
And back then,
I didn't know anything.

I feed a cat
with cat food,
I am happy,
The cat may not be

I become friends
with someone
through gifts
and compliance,
I am happy,
Someone says,
I don't know.

I run at the seaside,

Sea water wets my pants,
It starts raining,
Rainwater
Wets
my eyes.

I am soaked,
I open the door,
And I Hear
the sound of mother
breaking a bowl,
Startled.

Mother says,
Breaking things
is a good thing.

On the table,
Dinner is prepared,
I eat a lot,
Mother says,

Watching you eat the food I made,
I feel happy.

Finally,
I reply:
I am happy too.

与水有关

1. 杭州之初

我坐在母亲的车子里
车子绕着西湖
风景在变
变到杨公堤

我期侍车子上石拱桥
上去
又下去
就像坐过山车

茶林
村庄
寺院
亭子

母亲说
车子是移动的学校
她喜欢绕着西湖
给我
讲故事

关于
春天的桃花

夏天的莲子
秋天的梧桐树
冬天的断桥

关于白娘子
雷锋塔
苏小小
以及灵隐寺

我趴在窗户上
看着车外的风景
车转
风景在转
故事也在转

我记得
岳庙
北山路
以及叫新新的
饭店

这些，时而明亮，
时而模糊
是我七岁前的
片断

With Water

1. Hangzhou

Each time going up a bridge,
Anticipation courses through me,
Up,
Then down,
Like a rollercoaster ride.
Driving around XiHu,
The lake's panorama shifts,
The mountain's scenery transforms.

Tea plantations,
Villages,
Temples,
Pavilions.

Mom believes,
A car is a mobile school.
She enjoys sharing

Stories with me,
As we make laps around XiHu.

Tales of willows and spring blossoms,
Summer's lotus seeds,
Fall's plane trees,
And winter's broken bridge.

White Snake,
Leifeng Pagoda,
Longjing Tea,
Lingying Temple.

Leaning against the window,
Gazing at the changing scenery,
The car turns,
My view whirls,
My story also spins.

2. 曼哈顿的湖

曼哈顿之中
有个中央公园
公园之中
有一个大湖
以杰奎琳肯尼迪
命名

最初
我跟着母亲
绕湖散步
春天大片的樱花
秋天掉在湖边小道上的
野苹果
冬天的雪景
夏天湖上的水鸭

初中时
我开始跑步
独自戴着耳机绕湖奔跑

跑在音乐与风景里

一直跑
跑到眼里似无风景
耳边似无音乐
只有自己的呼吸声

以及
脚步声
一圈又一圈
一季又一季
跑到了我的十七岁

2. Manhattan

The lake water glistening,
I recall
The hazy snapshots of my 7-year-old memories.
Manhattan,
Central Park.
Jacqueline Kennedy,
A reservoir,
Named after Jacqueline Kennedy.

We stroll around the reservoir,
Our sights tinged pink with spring's cherry blossoms,
Inhaling the fragrance of wild apples,
Covered by winter's white blankets,
Accompanied by the duck noises.

Later,
Running laps in solitude,
Listening to the same song on repeat
Until I get sick of it.

In the realm of music and my scenic vista,
I keep running,
Until there is no longer music,
No longer a view.

Just my own breath,
And the rhythmic sound of my steps.
One more lap.
One more season.
Then comes my 17.

3. 特拉维夫的海

每天坐校车
穿过长长的海岸
左边是沙滩
右边是城市

看到太阳从海上
升起
看到太阳从海上
落下

我在地中海里
游泳
冲浪
感受着
洁净的阳光

我浮在死海里
什么都不做
就浮着

因为它是死海

在红海里
我学习潜水
那完全是
另一个世界
即寂静
又灿烂

就如我
即将到来的
十八岁

3. Tel Aviv

The bus ride to school,
Passesbythe long ocean coastline.
To the left was sand,
To the right was city.

I
Watch the sunrise from the sea,
Watch the sunset to the sea.

I'm unfamiliar with the sea.
My father takes me swimming,
Takes me surfing.
Slowly taking in,
Enjoying,
This Mediterranean Sea.

Floating,
I don't need to do anything,
Just float,
In the dead sea.

I started scuba diving,
In the Red Sea.
Once,
And once more,
Lost in another world,
Of quietness,
Of brilliance.
Of another world.

今天会下雨么

很长一段时间
我每周都会去中央公园做义工
每次都会在
同一个地方
遇见
同一个老妇人

体面的
优雅的
平静的
坐在
七十二街
公园入口处的
长椅上

有时捧着书
有时牵着狗
有时织手套
有时什么都不做
只是

长久地
看着
每一个路过她的人

有一天
经过她身边时
她突然开口问我：
今天会下雨么

Will it rain today

For a long time,
I would do volunteer work in Central Park
And each time,
At the same place,
I would meet the same old lady

Dignified
Elegant
Tranquil
Sitting on a bench,
At the entrance to Central Park,
on 72nd street.

Sometimes holding a book,
Sometimes holding her dog's leash,
Sometimes knitting a glove,
Sometimes not doing anything.
Just

Sitting there.
Watching each pedestrian that passes by.

One day,
When I was passing by,
She suddenly asked:
Will it rain today?

在沙漠

我蹲下来
触摸你
野玫瑰
开在沙漠里的红唇

我站着
倾听你
在旷野里
回响的风

我坐下来
在葡萄园下
闻到
酒的芬芳

我躺下来
与沙漠融为一体

头伸向
远古的海
脚趾触到
永恒的月光

In the desert

I crouch down,
Touching you,
Wild rose,
Red lips blooming in the desert.

I stand,
Listening to you,
Echoing through the wilderness,
The wind's resonance.

I sit down,
Beneath the vineyard,
Inhaling the fragrance,
Of intoxicating wine.

I lie down,
Merging with the desert.

My head reaches
Toward the ancient sea,
Toes touching,
Eternal moonlight.

酒吧

妈妈与女朋友吃饭

带上了我

我叫她苹果阿姨

苹果阿姨有一家自己的餐厅

还有一家酒吧

我很好奇

酒吧

啊！

酒吧！

母亲说

你还不够年龄

不能去酒吧

苹果阿姨看着我

神秘地笑

等会

我带你去

晚餐后

我们走去

酒吧

天空下起了雨

雨让一切变得神秘
并且沉重
走了很久
我们到了酒吧
阿姨对门口的保安说
让这小姑娘进去看看
酒吧
在地下一层
我忐忑地走了下去
四处看看
除了喝酒聊天的人
我什么都没有看到
从酒吧出来
雨
还在飘
我知道
我已经去过了酒吧
没什么特别
就像大人们的世界

BAR

Mom and her girlfriend dining,
They brought me along.
I call her Auntie Apple.
Auntie Apple owns her own restaurant
And also a bar.
I'm curious,
About the bar.
Oh!
A bar!
Mom says,
"You're not old enough,
You can't go to the bar."
Auntie Apple looks at me,
Smiles mysteriously,
"Later,
I'll take you."
After dinner,
We head to the bar.
Rain starts falling from the sky,
Making everything mysterious
And heavy.

Walking for a while,
We arrive at the bar.
Auntie tells the bouncer at the entrance,
"Let this little girl have a look."

The bar,
Is on the underground floor.
I nervously go down,
Look around,
Apart from people drinking and chatting,
I see nothing else.

Coming out of the bar,
Rain
Is still falling.
I know
I've been to the bar.

Nothing special,
Just like the world of adults.

宠物的命运

你是我的宠物
每天，每夜
我无比珍爱你
睡觉前，我会道
晚安
起床时
我会说，
早安

我珍爱你
像珍爱我的冰箱
我的床
我的枕头

有一天
我抱着你去公园
玩游戏
回家时
我忘了带回你

我弄丢了你
哭了几天后
我慢慢习惯了
另一个宠物
一只和你长得一模一样的
布娃娃

但我因此有了
忧伤
因为懂得了
宠物的
命运

Life of Pets

You are my pet,
Every day, every night,
I cherish you immensely.
Before sleeping, I'll say,
Goodnight,
Upon waking,
I'll say,
Good morning.

I treasure you,
Like I treasure my refrigerator,
My bed,
My pillow.

One day,
I took you to the park,
We played games,
But on the way home,
I forgot to bring you back.

I lost you.
After crying for days,
I slowly adapted
To another pet,
A doll that looks just like you.

But in doing so,
I gained a sense of sorrow,
For I understood
The fate of a
Pet.

我怕认错你

外婆
我们有五年没见了
我如果出现在
你每天要经过的小巷
你还能认出我么
外婆说
我怕认错你
太多与你一样大的姑娘
每天放学
从我身边嘻笑着经过
我时常错以为
她们就是
你
外婆
我不会认错你
我一生下来
你的脸
就印在了我的脑海里
外婆说
你的脸一直在变

从一岁变到七岁
从七岁到十二岁
十二岁夏天，
你与我挥手告别
然后就到了今年的
十七岁
外婆
夏天
我去看你
让你抚触我
十七岁的脸
外婆笑声灿烂
耳朵不好的她在电话里大声问
你想吃什么
我的宝贝
外婆
我想你的拥抱
以及你的红烧豆腐
我同样大声回答

I'm afraid of mistaking you

Grandma
It's been five years since we last met
If I were to appear
In the narrow alley you traverse daily
Would you still recognize me?
Grandma says
I'm afraid of mistaking you
So many girls your age
Every day after school
Giggling as they pass by me
I often mistakenly believe
That they are
You.
Grandma,
I won't mistake you
Since the day I was born
Your face
Has been imprinted in my mind.
Grandma says
Your face has been changing

From one to seven
From seven to twelve
In the summer at twelve
You waved goodbye to me
And now you've reached
Seventeen this year
Grandma
In the summer
I'll come to see you
Let you touch
The face of seventeen
Grandma's laughter is radiant
Her hearing impaired,
she loudly asks over the phone,
"What do you want to eat, my dear?"
Grandma,
I want your hugs
And your braised tofu!
I replied as loudly.

西瓜

院子里
种下一棵西瓜秧苗
是我新的思念

它开出了第一朵
花
金黄色的
就如月亮身边
最大的那颗星星
照进我的眼睛

第一朵
耀眼的花
没有结出果实
在不被看见的地方
另一朵花
结出了西瓜

在暗处开花的
虽耀眼不到别人的眼睛
却
都有属于自己的
真实
故事

Watermelon

In the garden,
Planted a recent watermelon sprout
My new yearning.

It bloomed a new flower.
Flower,
Shimmering gold,
Like the bright star,
Next to the moon,
Shining in my eyes.
Shrinking my pupils.

Another flower,
Grows where no man sees.
Growing in the shadows,
Shielded by shadows.
Unable to illuminate one's eyes,
Yet,
It has a story,
A story of their own.

明月

夕阳下去了
沙滩上
剩下我

夜深了
海鸟
飞走了

海上的波涛
印着明月

是昨天的明月
也是
三千年前的明月

我
又小又孤独的人类
走在明月里

Bright Moon

The sunset fades,
Along the shore,
Solitude becomes my company.

As night deepens,
Seabirds depart,
Leaving me alone.

The sea's waves,
Stamped by the radiant moon.

It's the moon from yesterday,
And also,
The moon of three millennia past.

I,
A diminutive and solitary soul,
Stroll beneath the luminous moonlight.

我也会老去

今天是星期一
是普通的一天
也不是普通的一天
因为
再过几个小时
我就十七岁了

街头很多人
第五大道上
长长的
游行的队伍
如游动的
龙

今天
是一个节日
哥伦布节

有点冷
我坐在出租车

看到一对牵着手
弓着背
相扶着
走进超市的老人
他们真的很老了
可他们也曾经有过
他们的
十七岁

十七岁后
我会一点点老去
老成他们的样子
他们已经经历过的时光
是我将要经历的

I will also grow older

Today is Monday
Just a normal day
But not just a normal day
Because
After a few hours
I will be 17

There are many people on the streets
On Fifth Avenue
Spectating the
Parade groups
Who are traversing through the streets
Like a dragon

Today
Is a holiday

The weather is cold
I sit in the taxi

Looking at a couple
Holding hands
Slightly slouched
Holding onto each other
Walking into the supermarket
Looking generations older
But
Only a few decades ago,
They enjoyed,
Their own
17

After a few more decades,
I will also grow older
Just like them
Go through what they've already experienced
Their past
Will be my future

三天

我喜欢你
我不用看着你
就知道
你已经在眼前
很近
近到能听见你心脏的声音
很远
远到无法触及

我喜欢你
我的双眼里有吻，封住你的唇
如同鲜花
充盈了春天
如同
美好的事物
充满了我的灵魂

我喜欢你
你是梦里的那只飞鸟

你是黑夜里的星星
你是树上的青苹果

我喜欢你
是寂静的，好像你并不存在
是沉默的
我在沉默中与你说话
我的沉默如水一般清澈
我的沉默如星星一样
遥远而明亮

我喜欢你
仿佛你已经离开
仿佛你已经老去
我喜欢你
远远的
热烈的
仅仅
只喜欢了三天

3 days

I like you

I don't need to look at you

Just know

You are already in front of my eyes

Very close

Close enough to hear the sound of your heart

Very far

Far enough to be out of reach

I like you

In my eyes, there are kisses, sealing your lips

Like flowers

Filling the spring

Like

Beautiful things

Filling my soul

I like you

You are the flying bird in my dream

You are the star in the night
You are the green apple on the tree

I like you
It's quiet, as if you don't exist
It's silent
I speak to you in silence
My silence is as clear as water
My silence is like stars
Distant and bright

I like you
As if you have already left
As if you have grown old
I like you
From afar
Passionately
Just
for three days

所有人，都曾经如此

母亲总一个人去
咖啡店写作看书
那天
她带着我去了

她说
当我怀你的时候
就想着有一天
我们一起
去咖啡馆

在咖啡馆
我第一次
用勺子吃糖
白色的小瓷瓶里
棕色的沙糖
太甜了
我记住这个甜
虽然那年

我只有三岁

在纽约
家对面
也有一家咖啡馆
我第一次
知道，咖啡是苦的
那年
我七岁

母亲不怎么会做饭
但她拍下了
很多
我赞美她做的
蛋炒饭的
视频

有年冬天
母亲生病了

我拍下了许多
她赞美我做的
虾仁鸡蛋面的视频

这天，
我在咖啡馆做作业
我点了杯酸奶与香草混合在一起的饮料
母亲在我对面看书
我让她品尝饮料的味道
她说
非常难喝

我从小挑食，
却一直有自己的怪口味
除了母亲的鸡蛋炒饭

临座的年轻妈妈
给她可爱的女儿

喂面包
母亲问
几岁了
年轻妈妈笑着回
三岁

我说，
这孩子笑得真好看
最干净最靠近天使的笑容
母亲说
所有人
都曾经如此

Everyone was like this once

Mother always goes alone
to the coffee shop
writing and reading alone
but that day
she took me along.
She said,
When I was carrying you
I always thought that one day
we would go together
to a café.

In the café
I, for the first time
used a spoon to eat sugar
in a small white porcelain bottle
brown sugar
too sweet
I remember this sweetness
Even though that year,

I was only three.
In New York
across the street from our home
there's another café
I, for the first time
learned that coffee is bitter.
That year,
I was seven.
Mother isn't good at cooking
but she recorded
many videos
of me praising her for
her fried rice.
One winter,
mom fell ill.
I recorded many videos
of the shrimp and egg noodles
she praised me for making.

One day
I'm doing homework in the café
I ordered a drink with yogurt
and honey mixed together
mom is reading across from me
I let her taste the drink
She says,
It tastes awful.

I've been a picky eater since childhood
but I always had my own strange taste
except for Mother's egg fried rice.

The young mom next to us
feeds her adorable daughter bread
Mother asks,
How old is she?
The young mom smiles and replies,
Three years old.

I say,
This child smiles so beautifully
The cleanest, closest to an angelic smile.
Mother says,
Everyone
Was like that once.

🐾 作者简介

Mandy Oren，2006年生，喜欢跑步与数学，热爱潜水与艺术，享受烹饪与阅读。偶尔写诗（在《十月》、《青年文学》、《江南》等杂志发表并获奖）。

Mandy Oren, born in 2006, is an avid runner, home cook and reader. She also enjoys mathematics, scuba diving, and art. Occasionally, she writes poetry（published and awarded in magazines such as "October," "Youth Literature", and "Jiangnan"）.

www.ingramcontent.com/pod-product-compliance
Lightning Source LLC
Chambersburg PA
CBHW051325120626
46547CB00015B/2401